Circus

Circus Performers

Denise M. Jordan

Heinemann Library
Chicago, Illinois

Customer Service 888-454-2279
Visit our website at www.heinemannlibrary.com

Designed by Sue Emerson, Heinemann Library
Printed and bound in the U.S.A. by Lake Book

06 05 04 03 02
10 9 8 7 6 5 4 3 2 1

Library of Congress Cataloging-in-Publication Data
Jordan, Denise M.
    Circus performers / Denise Jordan.
        p. cm. — (Circus)
Includes index.
Summary: Introduces various types of performers and their roles in the circus.
    ISBN: 1-58810-542-3 (HC), 1-58810-750-7 (Pbk.)
    1. Acrobats—Juvenile literature. 2. Circus performers—Juvenile literature. [1. Acrobats. 2. Circus performers.] I. Title.
    GV551 .J67 2002
    791.3'4—dc21

                        2001004790

Acknowledgments
The author and publishers are grateful to the following for permission to reproduce copyright material:
p. 4 Joanna B. Pinneo/Aurora/PictureQuest; p. 5 Pictor International, Ltd./PictureQuest; p. 6 Elena Rooraid/PhotoEdit/PictureQuest; p. 7 C. Smedley/Trip; p. 8 E. R. Degginger/Color Pic, Inc.; p. 9, 12 Jane Faircloth/Transparencies, Inc.; pp. 10, 16 Eugene G. Schulz; p. 11 Joel Dexter/Unicorn Stock Photos; pp. 13, 17 N & J Wiseman/Trip; pp. 14, 21 National Geographic Society; p. 15 Linda Rich/dancepicturelibrary.com; p. 18 Greg Williams/Heinemann Library; p. 19 Jeff Greenberg/Unicorn Stock Photos; pp. 20, 22 Roland Raith

Cover photograph courtesy of Jane Faircloth/Transparencies, Inc.

Every effort has been made to contact copyright holders of any material reproduced in this book. Any omissions will be rectified in subsequent printings if notice is given to the publisher.

Special thanks to our advisory panel for their help in the preparation of this book:

Eileen Day, Preschool Teacher
Chicago, IL

Paula Fischer, K–1 Teacher
Indianapolis, IN

Sandra Gilbert,
Library Media Specialist
Houston, TX

Angela Leeper,
Educational Consultant
North Carolina Department
of Public Instruction
Raleigh, NC

Pam McDonald, Reading Teacher
Winter Springs, FL

Melinda Murphy,
Library Media Specialist
Houston, TX

Helen Rosenberg, MLS
Chicago, IL

Anna Marie Varakin,
Reading Instructor
Western Maryland College

The publishers would also like to thank Fred Dahlinger, Jr., Director of Collections and Research at the Circus World Museum in Baraboo, Wisconsin, and Smita Parida for their help in reviewing the contents of this book.

Some words are shown in bold, **like this.**
You can find them in the picture glossary on page 23.

Contents

What Are Circus Performers?

Circus performers are people who are good at doing tricks.

Some **juggle**.

high wire

Others **tumble** on the ground.

Some walk on a **high wire**.

Where Do Circus Performers Work?

Circus performers work at the circus.

Some circus performers work inside.

Others work outside.

Circus performers help make
the circus fun.

What Do Trapeze Artists Do?

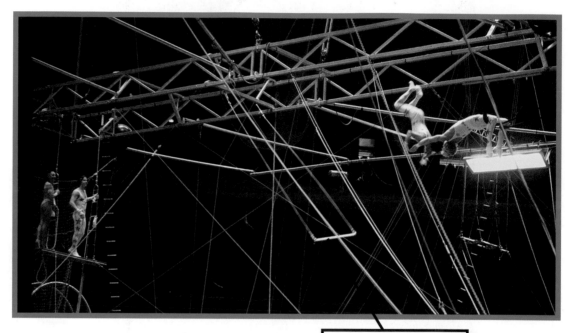

trapeze

Some **trapeze** artists swing from one trapeze to another.

They twist and turn their bodies as they fly through the air.

Trapeze artists are very strong.

What Do High Wire Artists Do?

High wire artists walk on a high, thin wire.

They are far above the ground.

high wire

They use long poles to help them stay up.

Some high wire artists do tricks on the wire.

What Do Acrobats Do?

Acrobats do tricks and flips on the ground.

teeterboard

They use **teeterboards** to spring into the air.

They can land on another acrobat's shoulders.

What Do Jugglers Do?

Jugglers keep lots of things in the air at one time.

They can move around while they **juggle**.

Some jugglers can juggle people!

What Do Riders Do?

Riders do tricks on horses.

They can stand on a moving horse.

pad

Some of the horses wear **pads.**

The pads help the riders stay up.

How Do People Learn to Be Circus Performers?

Some performers grow up in the circus.

They learn from other performers.

Some performers start in gymnastics.

When they grow up, they join
the circus.

How Do Circus Performers Keep Safe?

safety net | rope

Circus performers do their tricks over and over.

Some practice with **safety nets** and ropes.

Ropes keep them from falling.

Nets can catch them.

Quiz

Here are some things that you can see at the circus.

Can you name them?

Look for the answers on page 24.

?

?

?

Picture Glossary

acrobats
pages 12, 13

safety net
page 20

high wire
pages 5, 10, 11

teeterboard
page 13

juggle
pages 4, 14, 15

trapeze
pages 8, 9

pad
page 17

tumble
page 5

Note to Parents and Teachers

Reading for information is an important part of a child's literacy development. Learning begins with a question about something. Help children think of themselves as investigators and researchers by encouraging their questions about the world around them. Each chapter in this book begins with a question. Read the question together. Look at the pictures. Talk about what you think the answer might be. Then read the text to find out if your predictions were correct. Think of other questions you could ask about the topic, and discuss where you might find the answers. Assist children in using the picture glossary and the index to practice new vocabulary and research skills.

Index

Answers to quiz on page 22

trapeze

trapeze artist

safety net